MEMORIES THAT RELATES YOUR HAPPY LIFE

HAPPY LIFE

ARYAN SHARMA

Life.....

Life is a single word with many different connotations and meanings. Above all, life is about more than just being; it's also about how one defines that existence. As a result, it's vital to think about life from several angles. Philosophers, academics, poets, and authors have written extensively about what it means to live and, more significantly, what are the essential elements that characterize one's existence. This exercise has, of course, been done in a variety of ways. While philosophers sought to understand the meaning and purpose of people's lives, poets and authors recorded the diversity of life at various times. As a result, life is likely to be more than exciting.

Tough Life-

The adventure of living in the path of life. We are born, live our lives, and eventually pass away with time. We are attempting to shape our lives in this way. Everyone's life is different. Some people have a lot of problems in life, while others do not. Those who have never faced adversity in their lives have one perspective on life. Those that struggle in life have a different perspective. Life is frequently described as priceless. The various ways in which people seek to save lives reveal this even more clearly.Every day, doctors and scientists try to discover innovative treatments that will help people live longer lives. Life is full of both joys and disasters. The ups and downs of life are what they're called. Without them, life is just a never-ending war that can be won at any time. To overcome one's grief, it is necessary to find happiness in one's life. Only then does life appear to be lovely? Life is beautiful but not always easy, it has problems, too, and the challenge lies in facing them with courage, letting the beauty of life act like a balm, which makes the pain bearable, during trying times, by providing hope

Happiness, sorrow, victory, defeat, day-night are the two sides of the me coin. Similarly life is full of moments of joy, pleasure, success and comfort punctuated by misery, defeat, failures and problems. There is no human being on Earth, strong, powerful, wise or rich, who has not experienced, struggle, suffering or failure.

No doubt, life is beautiful and every moment – a celebration of being alive, but one should be always ready to face adversity and challenges. A person who has not encountered difficulties in life can never achieve success.

Difficulties test the courage, patience, perseverance and true character of a human being. Adversity and hardships make a person strong and ready to face the challenges of life with equanimity. There is no doubt that there can be no gain without pain. It is only when one toils and sweats it out that success is nourished and sustained.

Thus, life is and should not be just a bed of roses; thorns are also a part of it and should be accepted by us just as we accept the beautiful side of life.

The thorns remind one of how success and happiness can be evasive and thus not to feel disappointed and disheartened rather remember that the pain of thorns is short-lived, and the beauty of life would soon overcome the prick of thorns.

Those, who are under the impression that life is a bed of roses are disillusioned soon and become victims of depression and frustration. One who faces difficulties with courage and accepts success without letting it go to its head is the one who experience real happiness, contentment and peace in life.

Those, who think, that good times last forever, easily succumb to pressure during difficulties. They do not put in required hard work and efforts because they break down easily.

You can take the example of a student, who burns the mid night oil, makes sacrifices and resists temptations so that he can perform well. Similarly, a successful executive has to face the ups and downs of life, not forgetting that life is a mix of success and failure, joy and sorrow.

If he loses hope during difficult times, he would not achieve success and would be replaced by others. Even the strongest Kings and Emperors have had their cup of woes.

Life has not been a bed of roses for them. The adage 'Uneasy lays the head that wears the crown' has been rightly used for people, who are successful and are enjoying power and authority.

To sum up, life is beautiful just as roses but it has challenges which are like thorns and have to be faced and overcome by all. Those, who accept these, challenges and succeed, are the ones, who know how to live life in its true sense. Thus, enjoy life but also be prepared to bear the pricks of pain.

True Values of Life

We are surrounded by various kinds of lives around us. There are billions of other species including plants, animals, insects, birds, amphibians, etc. Each and every life, no matter how minuscule it is, is important, having its own value and contributes to the ecosystem in its own way. But, human life is considered more valuable than others, because of some distinct qualities that add value to existence.

To understand the true worth of human existence we should look at life from a different perspective, other than just eating, working, and living. The true value of life lies in protecting others and helping them. Fortunately, humans are gifted with exceptional intellect and brain along with dexterity, like no other creature on the planet. Only humans have the ability to help each other as well as other living creatures, in times of need. This is the greatest value that human life holds.

In other words, the true value of life lies in how much value does it holds for others. Consider the example of a tree that has been sheltering way farers from sun and rain for decades. The life of that tree is certainly valuable. Similarly, our life also gains more value if it is spent like the tree, in the service of others and spreading love and care.

How to Add Value to Life?

Now that we know what the true worth of life is, we will now discuss the changes that we could adopt to make our lives more valuable. Adding value to life is nothing but a change of attitude – you just have to change the way you look at others and perceive things. Below are some changes that you can adopt to add value to your life.

1) Become an Extrovert

Don't just keep up to yourself, rather reach out to others. Connect with them and know their problems, aspirations, etc. Talk to your neighbors and socialize. The more you socialize the more value will be added to your existence.

2) Give Respect

Another way to make your life more valuable is to give respect to everyone - young or old, rich or poor, strong or weak. When you treat everyone with respect, you will not only make your life worth for them but also earn respect from others.

3) Be Considerate and Supportive

You should always be considerate towards the suffering and needs of others; not only humans but animals as well. Help them, support them, and be compassionate towards their problems.

4) Value Other Lives as Well

The more you value other lives, the more value will be added to your own. It is a give and take relationship. From other lives I mean, all other life forms including humans, animals, plants, birds, etc.

5) Become Courageous

A courageous person can stand up and speak up for his own life and others' as well. On the contrary, lack of courage means a life spend in despair and fear. Such a life will have no value for itself or for others.

Life also relates to Time..........

Time is as precious as money to us. It is often said that "Time is Money" and this is certainly true when it comes to our personal and professional lives. The value of time can never be underestimated and it is important to make the most of every minute we have. Time is something that can never be replaced or recovered once it is gone. We can never get back the time that has passed and this is why it is so important to be mindful of how we use it. Every moment is an opportunity to do something meaningful, to improve our lives or to help others. The key to maximising the value of our time is to manage it effectively. This means setting aside specific times of the day to focus on particular tasks and to ensure that we are not wasting time on activities that are not productive. Planning ahead and setting goals can help us to make the most of our time. One of the best ways to make the most of our time is to focus on the present moment. We should strive to be mindful of the time we have and to make the most of it. This means taking the time to enjoy life's simple pleasures, such as spending time with family and friends or just taking a few moments to relax. Time is a valuable resource, so it should be treated as such. We must appreciate and value the time we have in order to make the most of it. Valuing time is important because it can help us to achieve our goals, avoid procrastination, and make the most of every moment. Valuing time is also important because it helps us to prioritize our tasks and focus on what is important. We can better manage our time and energy when we value it and use it wisely. Valuing time is also important because it can help us to be more productive and efficient in our daily tasks. Time is one of the most valuable resources available to us and it is important to understand and value the time we have. Valuing time is important because it can help us to prioritize tasks, avoid procrastination, and make the most of every moment. To value time, it is important to prioritize tasks, set realistic goals, and create a schedule that works for you. Valuing time can help us to be more productive and efficient in our daily tasks and make the most of our limited time. I hope the above provided essay on Value of Time will be helpful for you to know the importance of time in your life...

Memories....

Time is one of the most valuable resources available to us and it is important to understand and value the time we have. Valuing time is important because it can help us to prioritize tasks, avoid procrastination, and make the most of every moment. To value time, it is important to prioritize tasks, set realistic goals, and create a schedule that works for you. Valuing time can help us to be more productive and efficient in our daily tasks and make the most of our limited time.

There are many memories in our lives, including beautiful memories that make us stronger, and other memories that contain a lot of pain and make us feel sad, especially if they are memories related to people we have lost.

In fact, there are memories that represent great meaning to us, as they are the best that happened to us in our lives, such as moments of success, or knowing someone else's feelings towards us.

Childhood memories are our most beautiful memories. They are engraved in our minds and hearts. I do not forget the kindness of my father and mother, their love for me, and the gifts they used to buy me. My beautiful toys I spent many times with her, playing with them and talking to them as if they could hear me, my little room, my bed and my desk.

I sat at this desk for several years studying my lessons, writing down my assignments, everything in my room had a fond memory in my mind and in my heart.

Memories of adolescence are among the beautiful memories that remain hidden inside us for life. At this stage, I had successful and failed experiences. It is the stage in which I rebelled against receiving orders from my parents, and tried to rely on myself and make difficult decisions.

Sometimes I made the right decisions, and other times I made the wrong ones, so it is important to consult our parents and benefit from their advice.

And there are people I love, but we parted because of education, or travel. These people are still present in my memory, and I cannot forget the beautiful times I spent with them. My memories of middle school and high school I can never forget, as they constitute the largest part of my memories, and at this stage I was exposed to many situations.

These situations are what formed my personality, this stage in which major changes occur in a person's life. Therefore, it is full of experiences and difficult situations, and this stage is when we make true friendships, and these friendships may last a lifetime.

Beautiful memories bring happiness to our souls, and improve our psychological state, and therefore we should remember the beautiful things in our lives, such as our living with the family, the mother's love, the father's kindness, spending quality time with brothers and sisters, adventures and trips, the places we went to with people we love, Every beautiful thing we lived in the past will make us happy when we remember it.

Many times we don't recall memories, but rather they come suddenly and we find ourselves smiling. A person carries within him the memories of a lifetime, and it is difficult for anyone to see them. They are special memories that provide you with feelings of love and happiness, and help you to continue progressing in life with some hope.

I like to remember all the beautiful things that happened to me in the past, they are my memories that I live by, and this does not mean that the present is bad, but the moments of happiness that we lived in the past are not repeated.

And some memories are painful and cause us some sadness, but we have benefited from it, and we are good to ourselves, our private memories are ours, and we should not talk about them with others. It is a summary of our experiences in life, we lived it honestly, and we learned from it, and in many cases we failed and tried again in order to reach success.

Have you ever wanted to know what someone was thinking or feeling in a given moment? Perhaps someone has, to all appearances, been feeling one way, but for some unexplainable reason you felt they were actually experiencing another emotion. It is possible that your subconscious was picking up on subtle clues in the other person's face, manner of speaking, or posture that gave away their true reaction to the situation ("Gut Feelings").

To most people, these feelings are only vague hunches that are often dismissed, but to people who have honed their instincts and have learned to interpret these visual signals for what they are, other people's true emotions become clearer. There are many subtle indications of what a person is thinking or feeling at a given time, which, when recognized, can be used to discern emotional reactions and detect lies.

The first and most obvious place one might look for insight into someone else's emotional state is the face. There are many obvious expressions on people's faces that we are accustomed to interpreting without thinking about it, smiling and frowning, for example. However, because these are so obvious, these are the expressions people will try to fake and will fake with reasonable success. Less apparent clues, however may be a better indication of what someone is feeling. For example, someone may crinkle their nose briefly when they dislike something, or begin to squint slightly when they are nervous or under tension (psychologytoday.com). Learning to recognize genuine smiles is also helpful in determining others' feelings. "Smiling is a big part of facial body language. As a general rule real smiles are symmetrical and produce creases around the eyes and mouth, whereas fake smiles.... Emotions are feelings that play an important part in human lives.

It allows humans to do many things such as understanding themselves and communicating with one another. Most importantly, emotions are mostly responsible for humans thoughts and actions. There are many types of emotions that you might want to have such as love, happiness, inspired, or proud. On the other hand, there are also negative emotions such as hopeless, lonely, or miserable which you would want to avoid or overcome if you have.... Emotion and reasoning are the two ways of knowing which work very well with types of areas of knowing which are science and art.

Whereas for ethic it is a completely different thing because they are contradictory to each other. That's the reason why human beings face such big setbacks on day to day basis. So which in more important in justifying moral disecions, reasons or emotions? In order to determine the relative importance of reason and emotion with regard to our morals, I will throw light on..

Emotions and feelings are some of the driving forces in our lives and essentially control our reactions, ideas, and choices. Emotions allow us to form connections with others, make decisions about the world around us, and provide us with the motivation to accomplish various tasks. However, emotions generally come with a lot of confusion and variability due to how differently people utilize and deal with them. One common emotion I feel that all people deal with, and handle differently is anxiety, EMOTIONS IN GENDER, CULTURE AND DIFFERENT AGES INTRODUCTION Emotion, being a very broad concept, it can be studied in various different aspects. The aspects have a very wide range right from emotions being connected to cognition till emotions being connected to social settings. Emotions generally refer to a complex psychological state that involves three distinct components: a subjective experience, a physiological response, and a behavioural or expressive response.. "Rational Thought & Emotions: The Internal Battle for Balance." Emotions are powerful, innate sensations that can control and influence numerous aspects of our lives from our actions to our mood and even our social relationships. Many believe that our emotions are an evolutionary mechanism designed to help an individual respond appropriately to the environment around them. Regardless of ones perspective on emotions, it is irrefutable how big of an influence emotions can have on an individual; especially.

Emotions No matter how hard you try, you cannot control your emotions, only attempt to hide them. Emotions influence every aspect of our lives, what we do, what we say, and et cetera. All of our emotions, from anger to insecurity, are influenced by several factors, just as our lives are influenced by our emotions (Gelinas, Emotions 35). First of all, it causes problems when one does not trust himself, and it shows up in many ways. Some people brag to call attention to themselves, causing, Emotion and Emotion Experience Emotional disturbances are very common in psychopathology, being present at a wide range of psychological conditions, such as mood disorders, anxiety disorders, impulse control disorders, personality disorders and sleep disorders.

Life After Death....

Afterlife is (in some religions) life after death. Those who feel that death is a positive factor in someone life may argue that there is an afterlife waiting for people, animals and all other living things in the world that are destined to become deceased. While others against death may argue that death is the final chapter in a person's life and there is nothing awaiting them afterwards. Dealing with the death of a loved one is one of life's most challenging obstacles. The pain and suffering that a person goes through cannot be fully understood unless experienced firsthand, like people that have experienced death through abortion. However, for some who have experienced death in war, death is something more like a game, where it is feared, yet made fun of in hopes of lessening the truth of reality. In the short story, "The Things They Carried"

Contents